movement games
for children of all ages

By

Esther L. Nelson

illustrations by
SHIZU MATSUDA

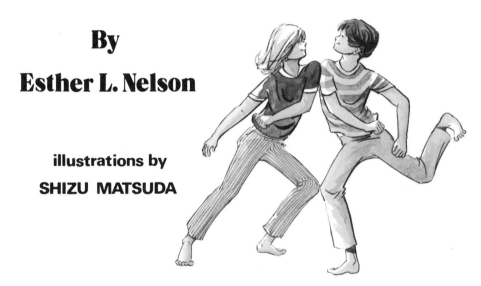

STERLING
PUBLISHING CO., INC. NEW YORK

Oak Tree Press Co., Ltd.
London & Sydney

Many thanks to Mara Sokolsky for her contribution of ideas and help with the writing of various sections, and ultimate thanks to my editor, Sheila Barry, without whom there would be no book. And to the thousands of young movers and shakers who were the joyful guinea-pigs for this book over a period of twenty years.

To L.M.L.

Third Printing, 1977

Copyright © 1975 by Esther L. NELSON
Published by Sterling Publishing Co, Inc.
419 Park Avenue South, New York 10016
Distributed in Canada by Saunders of Toronto, Ltd., Don Mills, Ontario
Distributed in Australia and New Zealand by Oak Tree Press Co., Ltd.,
P.O. Box J34, Brickfield Hill, Sydney 2000, N.S.W.
Distributed in the United Kingdom and elsewhere in the British Commonwealth
by Ward Lock Ltd., 116 Baker Street, London W 1
Manufactured in the United States of America
All rights reserved
Library of Congress Catalog Card No.: 74-31710
Sterling ISBN 0-8069-4530-3 Trade   Oak Tree 7061-2068-X
4531-1 Library
Distributed to the music trade by Belwin Mills Publishing Corp.

CONTENTS

3. DO AS I DO

4. PANTOMIME TRIPS 47

5. GROUP IMPROVISATIONS

6. AWARENESS GAMES

BEFORE YOU BEGIN

Movement is natural to children, and you won't have any trouble getting them to join in these games, but as you work through this book with the same group, you'll find exciting changes taking place. As the children learn to co-ordinate their movements, as they develop movement skills, begin to understand direction, level, rhythm, and dynamics, they will develop new feelings of confidence in themselves and their bodies. They will lose much of their self-consciousness and shyness, their ideas will flow more easily and they will become more inventive and creative.

Certainly, they will learn to concentrate for longer periods—not only on the games—but in other areas of their lives as well. Hopefully, they will work together more co-operatively and criticize others in a more constructive vein. Once they start creating in movement, the natural next step is to create in other disciplines. They can use the same techniques they learned in movement to help them with math, to do innovative work in art and music, in writing, acting, and other means of self-expression.

Where to Begin

Start with simple games and work up to more complicated ones. Age ranges, listed for each game, will give you an idea of where to begin. Each section starts with the easier games, and once you master them, the more complex co-ordinations follow. But use the age listings with caution and flexibility. Sophisticated four-year-olds may accomplish with ease what less-exposed five-year-olds spend weeks learning. Seven-year-olds who have developed a feeling for rhythm and movement may "out-think" the brainiest nines who haven't. Where the listing says 3-up or 5-up, that means there isn't any age limitation. College students play the games and enjoy them just as much as three-year-olds do, though they find other values in them—most of the time. Try them yourself!

Your Shoe, Your Pan and Your Orchestra

You can play almost every one of these games without music. You can clap, tap on the wall, table or desk, slap the floor with your shoe. If you have them, maracas, drums, and pots and pans are good for beating out rhythms. If you play the piano, guitar, or the autoharp, by all means, do it; music certainly adds dimension. If you have a phonograph, bring along the records you like most for background music. Your enthusiasm will automatically communicate itself to the group, so whether you love madrigals, bagpipes, electronic sound or gamelan ensembles, use them. You can only increase the children's sensitivity to the world, to themselves and to the arts.

Wait—

Before you start moving, get rid of shoes and stockings. When toes are free to feel the floor, moving is easier and much more fun. If a child is reluctant to take off shoes, don't insist. They will soon come off anyway, without urging.

Talk out and explain every game or movement ahead of time with the group. Bring out their ideas, get them concerned and involved in the subject at hand before you begin to move. This is the only preparation you'll need for most of the games.

From the very start, encourage the children to move each part of their bodies. Begin with fingers and call attention to how they bend and stretch, twist and turn. Add wrists and see what they can do. Elbows can move in many directions, and bend and stretch. Shoulders can rotate, shake and move up and down. Test the possibilities of head, toes, ankles, knees, hips, chest and back. Then try combinations, so that lying on the floor, you move only your fingers and toes, or only the fingers of your right hand and the toes of your left foot. Human bodies are not nearly as limited as you may think, and when you add imagination, all things are possible. Experiment! Invent! Explore!

Changing the Games

Vary the games as much as you want—change them in any way that works. They are only jumping-off points for you and the children. If you want to develop your own variations, take a look at the checklist "Ways to Invent Movement" on page 94 of this book. It shows seven basic techniques you can use to change or expand any activity so that it is almost unrecognizable! And within those seven methods lie thousands of variations. Keep alert to the suggestions which the children contribute, too. Try them. If they work, wonderful! If not, at least you respected the children enough to try out their ideas. Don't let them feel let down if they don't work—praise them for their contributions.

The children will request the games they like best again and again. Don't be afraid to repeat them. You can make each version different from the time before, and if you don't, the kids will.

Everybody Play

Children with handicaps, mental, physical, and emotional, can benefit just as much from movement games as "normal" kids do. Deaf children can play rhythm games (they feel the rhythm through vibrations—let them put their hands on the drum skin; they can watch the leader and join the beat); children in wheelchairs can stretch and bend and rotate many parts of their bodies; they can move their chairs in different floor patterns; blind children or children with visual impairment can respond to music and rhythm and images—just acquaint them with the limitations of the space they have to move in before you start. And everyone loves to act things out.

Movement is a process of discovery, of creation and invention. The games are springboards to the excitement of tangling with gravity, of travelling in space, of conquering it by jumping and leaping through it, by cutting it, changing it, distorting it. All the games are challenging; they have been tested and they all "work."

So—go to it and have fun. If you do, the children will, too!

1. RHYTHM GAMES TO BEGIN WITH

FIND YOUR OWN BEAT Ages 5-up

An introduction to the rhythm that beats in everything.

This is not so much a game as a way to begin working with rhythm. It is meant to start you off by tuning you in to yourself.

Take your own pulse. Use your second, third and fourth fingers to find the beat in your wrist; your thumb has a pulse of its own. If you can't find the rhythm in your wrist, put your fingers alongside your Adam's apple and find it in your neck.

Show your group how to do the same thing. When they really get the feel of it, ask them to tap their feet in time to their own "drummers," a tap each time they feel the beat.

Now have the children walk around the room in time with their own beats. Some children will have the same beat, and some beats will be slower or faster, or perhaps uneven. Encourage each child to walk in his or her own direction and pattern, too.

Then experiment with the rhythm. Run, and see what happens to it. As the group runs, heartbeats speed up and the rhythm gets faster. Ask them to keep time with the rhythm as they run, and remind them to move—not just in a circle—but weaving their own individual patterns.

WALK—RUN—GALLOP

This basic movement and rhythm game results in an immediate sense of achievement.

Clap a "walking rhythm" and get your group to clap it with you. Write it:

Play it on a drum or the bottom of a pot. Let the children take turns playing it. When they feel it in their bodies, walk it out all together, first in a line, then in a circle. Then lead the line into different shapes.

Write a run:

The walk and the run are both even rhythms, even though one is twice as fast as the other.

How about a skip or a gallop where the rhythm is uneven?

Clap out these different rhythms on the drum, or the pot, or even on the wall, and give the group a chance to identify the walking, running and galloping beats. Get them to clap with you. When they know the rhythms well, have them move to each, once around the room.

Name the corners of the room: one is the Walking Corner, one the Running Corner, and one the Galloping Corner. Then divide the group into three parts and send each to a different corner; the children in the Walking Corner become Walkers; the ones in the Running Corner are Runners; the last go to the Galloping Corner and become Gallopers.

When each group is sure of its identity, tell them, "Open up your ears and listen for your own rhythm!"

When the walking music or rhythm is played, Walkers stretch their arms out to the side, lift their knees and walk around the outside of the room, past the Gallopers, past the Runners and back to their own corner. When the Runners hear their rhythm, they stretch their arms out and run on their toes around the room; and of course the same with the Gallopers who gallop once around the room and return to their own corner.

When each group has had a turn, change parts. Walkers become Runners, Runners become Gallopers, Gallopers become Walkers. Each time they change parts, they must listen for their new rhythm. Make sure each group knows its new rhythm. Give each group the chance to do all three rhythms and movements.

More difficult and more fun:

The next time you play this game, try it another way: have each group move backwards around the room. Another day, change again; this time try the movement turning: walking and turning, running and turning, and galloping and turning.

With older children, try a skip instead of a gallop. It's a real challenge to skip and turn in a circle around the room.

Acting and play writing without words.

Once the group learns the basic movement rhythms, a world of possibilities opens up. Turn the rhythms into characters. The walking rhythm could become a parent taking a child to school; the running rhythm, the child. Since running is usually twice as fast as walking, the child must take twice as many steps as its parent and almost run in place alongside in order to keep up. The galloping rhythm can be a member of the mounted police galloping through the street to control traffic.

It helps to have the children clap out their parts, first separately, then all together, before they begin to "act."

Cast your play and write its plot. For a young group, keep to familiar events; for example: the parents take their children to school and return home. At school the children might join hands and skip in a circle, using the galloping rhythm. At 3 o'clock the parents return to fetch their children, while the mounted police direct traffic. The parents might be angry at their children and scold them as they walk along; the children might play pranks, kick stones, pick up leaves, and so on. Get them to use their own ideas for the personalities and activities of parent and child and they will enjoy themselves immensely. (You will also learn what goes on in their homes.) Be sure to change parts and give the parents a chance to be children.

Add characters if you want, such as a traffic cop. He or she stands tall and somber and signals to the cars to stop, with one hand, by stretching it straight out in front and flexing the wrist up, in a "stop" motion, and then beckoning with the other hand for the cars to come from the other direction. Done slowly and soberly, the rhythm would look like this:

Another rhythm play for young children may be Father or Mother coming home from work, driving the car slowly in heavy traffic, bumper-to-bumper, then speeding up as traffic clears, and going quite fast, so that the mounted policeman gallops alongside the car, stops it and writes out a ticket.

In another play, Father or Mother might take a child to the horse show on a motorcycle. They climb on, adjust their helmets, and speed down the deserted roadway (a brisk running step). At the horse show each owner holds the reins of a horse, leads him around the ring (proud walking steps), and then turns to the judges and bows. Parent and child applaud the show horses (double-fast running beat). They remount their motorcycle and ride home while the horses and their masters gallop home in the other direction.

The rhythms look like this:

Motorcycle

Walking horses

Applause

Galloping horses

For older children try a camping trip: start with a slow walk up the hill, with packs on backs. At the top, a swarm of mosquitoes attack, and the campers quickly swat them, as they buzz around in all directions. The campers pitch their tent on the top of the mountain and hammer nails into the ground with long slow movements, and then run down the other side of the slope to explore.

The possibilities for rhythm plays are endless. Let the children make up their own. If they need ideas, suggest they experiment with the circus, the zoo, the amusement park or miniature golf.

TALKING IN RHYTHM

(in your own words)

Ask the group, as you clap on each beat:

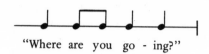

"Where are you go - ing?"

They can answer:

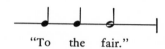

"To   the   fair."

Let them choose their own answers, and clap them back to you. Make sure each syllable gets a clap, so that if they answer "To the supermarket," it sounds like this:

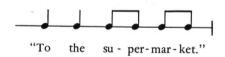

"To   the   su - per - mar - ket."

and not like this:

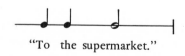

"To   the supermarket."

If the leader asks the questions, you can play this game with 4-year-olds, but 6- or 7-year-olds can ask and answer their own questions.

16

Sometimes it takes a while to understand that each syllable has its own clap, but once the group gets the idea, it is a great victory for listening, for understanding, and for translating a concept into rhythm.

The questions and answers in life can go on endlessly, and so can this game. The questions can be about anything: about parents, chores at home, friends, pets, and the answers don't have to be true. Everyone loves to clap out funny answers, and soon the children will realize they are having conversations, not only with words, but with beats. Suggest that they whisper the words and accentuate the rhythms, use loud and soft beats for variety and melody. At last they can drop the words altogether and talk with rhythm alone.

DRUM CONVERSATIONS

American Indians and African drummers have been doing it for centuries—the possibilities are unlimited.

You don't need actual drums for these conversations, though it's more fun to use them. The game works just as well with pots or rapping against the wall. First, let the children "talk in rhythm" with each other (see page 16) and then ask them to leave out the words altogether. Encourage them to go beyond just question rhythms now and try for more intricate patterns. Since the "drums" are engaging in "conversation," each drummer must listen carefully to what the other is saying, and respond in kind, just as he or she does when talking.

You can use this game when you're working on an American Indian or African project. Pass messages from tribe to tribe, about an on-coming wagon train or a fire on the prairie. Working in this way, the children really get the feel of the drum, and its enormous opportunities for self-expression. The conversations can be angry or playful, urgent or humorous. Let them experiment and explore the possibilities. It's fascinating to listen to two drummers talk and then ask the children to guess what was going on!

NAMES IN RHYTHM

Find the beat in your name.

Clap out a name in your group:

"My   name   is   Su - san."   "My   name   is   Eb - en - ee -zer."

Be sure to clap it in a natural speaking rhythm and not like this:

"My   name   is   Su - san."

As you clap out each name, the group can do it, too. Then choose one name and let the children walk it, which means stepping the rhythm with their feet, first in place and then around the room. Now vary the rhythm: slow it down, speed it up, run it, run the name backwards, spin it around and around.

Ask the children to work individually and create their own patterns for their own names. They can slink their names like tigers, fly them like vultures, inch them like snails. The children will have their own ideas about this after you suggest the theme. Then ask them to leave the name behind and use just its rhythm and movement.

Add the rhythm of the last name in another complete line and you will have a longer sequence to experiment with:

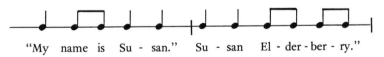

"My   name   is   Su - san."   Su - san   El - der - ber - ry."

When you work with older children, you can discuss the fact that we really don't talk this way; we speak faster, we speak differently depending on our circumstances. Explore those vocal patterns further. Try to make them real. This will lead to new rhythms, and make the children far more sensitive to movement and rhythm possibilities.

19

RHYTHM IN COLOR

Composing rhythm lines.

You don't have to know how to read music to compose your own rhythms, but once you learn to translate rhythm into symbols, it is much easier to learn to read notes. When you have moved to the different rhythms —walking, running, galloping—making them tangible is the next step and a simple one.

You'll need colored construction paper or similar pages which you color yourself. Regular notebook paper is good; the children can see it clearly and it is readily available. Start with half a dozen pages each of red, blue, green, and yellow.

Hold up a red paper and explain to the children that it represents a walking note. Now put three red papers on the floor, with a small space between them, and you have three walking notes. Clap this pattern out with the children, and say it as you clap it:

WALK-WALK-WALK

Ask one child to walk it out, while the other children say it and clap it.

Now place two green papers next to the red ones (all in one line). The green represents a running note, and you have added two of them to the three walking notes. Clap and say the rhythm:

WALK-WALK-WALK-RUN-RUN

When the children understand it, have them clap it and say it while they move around the room. When the children see the "notes," hear and feel the rhythm, and then translate it into movement, they learn the concept quickly.

Now introduce a blue paper. Blue is a slow note, take a giant step and then hold very still. Add another blue square. Now you have a pattern of

WALK-WALK-WALK-RUN-RUN-GIANT STEP-GIANT STEP

Give the children turns rearranging the colored papers so they can make their own rhythm patterns, while the rest of the group claps them out and moves to them.

More colors:

Another day add a yellow paper, which is a gallop. As the children add to their rhythm vocabulary they can create more and more interesting patterns, and will find it easy to go on to written notes.

WRITING RHYTHM

From "Row-Row" to popular jingles.

You'll need a piece of paper and pencil for each child. Ask the children to write their names at the bottom of the page so when it comes time to go home they will be sure to get their own papers. Then have them draw a line across the top third of the page, and show the children how to make a walking note: a circle around the line, filled in, with a stem along the right-hand side of the note. It looks like this:

Make four of those walking notes, and then a bar line to mark the end of the first measure (the space between two bar lines). It looks like this:

Ask the children to walk it out, and say it and clap it at the same time.

Draw eight walking notes:

If you connect them, two by two, across the tops of the stems, you'll have running notes. It will look like this:

Don't forget the bar line. Now run out the line you have just written.

Each time you write rhythms, try a new one. The giant step note looks the same as the walking note, but it is not filled in. It looks like this:

You can combine the notes into a song all the children know. Ask them to draw a new line across their papers and write two walking notes, two running notes, and one walking note in the first measure and then a bar line:

The next measure has four running notes, a giant step note and a bar line:

If you have a blackboard, write the two measures on it so the children can compare their work with yours. If not, write them on your own paper and hold them up for the children to see.

Then ask one of the children to clap out and say what is in the first measure—walk, walk, run run, walk. Ask a different child to clap and say the next one; then have everyone clap it together, say it and walk it out around the room while they read it. Don't let the children just memorize the rhythm; they need to look at their pages and read the notes so that they identify the written symbol with the rhythm.

When they have clapped out both measures, you can tell them they have written the rhythm of the first line of "Row, Row, Row Your Boat." They will be very impressed.

Very fast running notes are similar to regular running notes, but have two lines across the top connecting them. They look like this:

If you want to write just one running note, you add a tail to the stem like this:

As the children become more and more proficient writing rhythms, you can experiment with really complex patterns. Older children love them. Galloping rhythm is:

Here are some easy rhythm lines:

Fre - re Jac - ques, Fre - re Jac - ques, Dor-mez vous,   Dor-mez vous

Son - nez les ma - tin - es   Son - nez les ma - tin - es

Ding dong ding   Ding dong ding.

At the end of the last measure you place two bar lines, which means that it is the end. If you put two dots in front of the two bar lines, it means you repeat the section that comes before those dots. In other words, start again from the beginning.

24

Here's another:

Skip   skip   skip   to   my   Lou,   Skip   skip   skip   to   my   Lou,

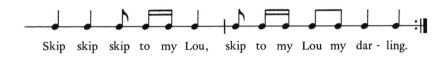

Skip   skip   skip   to   my   Lou,   skip   to   my   Lou   my   dar - ling.

Can you tell what this is?

Let the children write out the rhythm lines for popular jingles and see if the rest of the group can guess what they are. If you're working with older children, put that jingle rhythm line into movement.

It's "Waltzing Matilda."

25

2. PARTY GAMES PLUS

BALLOON BOUNCE

A wonderful way to get moving.

No one of any age can resist a balloon—holding it, throwing it, catching it, playing with it—and because it is so light and moves so slowly, it is easier to handle than a ball for a young child.

For these bounces, you will need enough balloons for all the children in the group, and a few extra to replace those that pop along the way.

Begin with three-year-olds. Give each one a balloon and tell them to throw the balloons in the air. When the balloons fall to the ground, ask the children to pick them up and, this time, try to catch the balloons *before* they land.

Now suggest that the children toss the balloons in the air and, as they come down, tap them up again. See how many times they can tap the balloons up without letting them touch the floor. Can they keep them bouncing three times, or six times?

Then it is an easy next step to tap the balloons back up with other parts of their bodies. They can use their heads, or their elbows, as well as their hands. They can even bend over after they throw them up and let the balloons bounce down on their backs. Let the children see how many times they can bounce their balloons with each different part.

Older children can hop on one foot and bounce the balloon on the other knee. They can lie on the floor and bounce the balloon with their feet. Let them experiment with using other parts of the body to keep the balloons afloat. Then ask them to count the number of times they can hit the balloon with head or hand or foot, without any interruptions. Can they do it more than twenty times?

HORSES HORSES HORSES

Lots of excitement.

You can play both of these games either as team relays or as ordinary speed races. The children take partners. One child is the horse, the other the rider.

PONIES

The Pony stands at one end of the room in front of the Rider, with arms extended to the back. The Rider holds the Pony's hands, and at your signal, they both gallop toward the other end of the room. Knees should be lifted high, and the arms of both Pony and Rider should be fully outstretched, at least at the beginning of the race. Later on, in the rollicking gallop, as they try for speed, you might have a few jockeys who are faster than their mounts! Point out that the riders should keep the same rhythm as the ponies, that will slow them down.

At the opposite wall, Pony and Rider must change roles: switch places, and reverse arm positions. This calls for a real switch in thinking, as well as physical co-ordination, so let them practice it ahead of time. Extending arms out to the back is an unusual position, and the Rider needs to take it quickly in order to become the Pony. When the switch is effected, each team gallops back to the starting place.

HORSES HORSES HORSES

TROTTERS

Use the same arm positions in this game, but now the Horse and Rider move differently. The Horse trots instead of galloping. A "trot" is a "prance"—a run with knees raised high in front. To make it more stylish, horses should point their toes.

In a real harness race, the rider, now the Driver, sits behind in a little wagon called a sulky, with legs up and stretched to the sides. In this game, the Driver runs in a similar position, with knees straight and toes pointed, kicking out his or her legs on a diagonal on either side of the trotting Horse.

Let the children practice the movements individually. They will be changing parts in this game, too, so they both need to know each movement. Then let the partners practice racing together. The combination of prance and run-kick is great fun to do, but because there is so much more to remember when the children change rôles, it is better to use this game with older children.

Start at one end of the room, as with the other race, change parts at the opposite wall, and return to the starting place to win, place and show.

DOG DASH

Funny and good for you, too.

The group lines up in two or more teams, as if for an ordinary relay. Explain that now they are Dogs and have four legs, so they must use all four of them to run with. Make sure they understand that dogs run on their *feet* and not on their *knees*.

At your signal, the first Dog from each team runs to the opposite wall. There it must turn its back to the wall and wag its tail three times while counting aloud "One—Two—Three!" to make sure it gets all the wags in. The Dog gets up on its hind legs to do the wag, which provides a needed breather. Then, on all fours, the Dog races back to its team, faces the next Dog on line, wags another "One—Two—Three" count, and goes to the end of the line. On count "Three" the next Dog starts running.

It is tiring to run on four legs for a long distance so don't make the dash-track more than 20 feet long.

30

PIG ROLL

Hilarious—and more difficult than you think.

Line up the group in teams, as if for a relay race, but leave plenty of room between lines. The children are Pigs and they are going to *roll* to the pigpen. The first Pigs on each line lie on the floor, parallel to the opposite wall. Their arms rest on the floor too, but stretch overhead.

At your signal, the Pigs start rolling across the room to the pigpen. Rolling one way is enough for younger children, but older ones can roll back, too. The trick is to roll straight; generally, as the children roll, their bodies turn and they go off course. Each Pig must touch the opposite wall with its entire body (which means its body must be straight), before it can start rolling back.

If the Pigs are rolling both ways, the returning Pig must roll into and *touch* the next child who is waiting (in rolling position) on line. Then the first Pig jumps up to make way as the newly-bumped Pig starts rolling to the pigpen.

LETTING THE AIR OUT

A game of observation and imagination, especially enjoyed by young children.

Untie an air-filled balloon, but hold it by the neck; throw it up in the air, and see what happens. It does a wild dance of its own, dipping, twisting, turning, shooting, as the air goes out. Experiment with several balloons—observe them. Each one moves differently. Ask the children to describe the movements of the balloons in words. Talk about the shape and directions the movements take, and try to find vivid language—swoops and swerves, spurts and zooms and zips.

Then, when the children are actively involved, ask them to be balloons that lose their air. Choose a few children at a time to "let their air out," and suggest that the others watch and develop new ideas to use when their turns come. Remind the "balloons" that every part of them must move, that nothing can be left behind or just drag along. Keep using the descriptive words that the children have contributed. They will help to keep the movements fresh and lively.

MUSICAL BUMPS

"Musical Chairs" with more pizzaz and less furniture.

Play whatever music you choose on the piano, guitar, autoharp, or from a tape—or don't use music at all—just clap. The contestants move to the rhythm through the entire room. When you stop the music or stop clapping, everyone must sit on the floor. The last person to sit is O-U-T, and must go to the sidelines with the leader. For a "sit" to be considered "safe," the contestant's bottom must touch the floor.

Vary the type of music or rhythm so that some is loud, some soft, some fast, some with a jazz beat. The type of movement should change as the rhythm changes without your having to say a word. Vary the length of each segment, too, so that the contestants are totally unprepared for the moment the sound stops. Use a few very short segments; they make the game exciting, and train the children to listen.

If the music is on tape or record, change the volume control suddenly. Many children will sit down at the change in dynamics, without realizing the music is still playing and the game is still going on.

When there are just two children left, they will be busy watching each other, and you may have one tie after another, as they both hit the floor at the same time. If this happens, ask them to close their eyes while they move to the music, and use their entire bodies, each part that can bend, rotate, stretch, extend and contract. You'll soon have a winner.

Musical Bumps Backwards:

When you have played the game through once or twice, reverse it. Start everyone on the floor. First discuss the possibilities for movement, even in one spot. There are twists, turns, kicks and reaches, for example. No one is allowed to get up on his or her knees, because that is a shortcut to standing, which is what everyone must do when the music stops. The last child to stand is O-U-T.

After you play Musical Bumps Backwards twice or perhaps three times, the winners compete against each other to select a champion, who bows to the group while everyone applauds—a good note to end on.

BIRTHDAY PRESENTS

Special for birthdays and Christmas.

The birthday "presents" enjoy this game as much as the birthday child. Play it to celebrate the birthdays of children in the group.

Give the children a few minutes to think of a present they would like to give the birthday child, but they must not reveal it. There is no limit to what it may cost. Anything is possible—from diamonds that sparkle, shimmer and shine, to a plane that zooms up from the airport, flies through space and comes in for a safe landing. Once they decide on a present, the next thing to do is to decide how to act out the movements for it. If they choose a doll, they need to perform stiff movements. If they choose a dog, they could chase their tails around in a circle, give a paw or roll over with paws up in the air.

Consult with each child as he or she works out the movements, offer suggestions and help, and you may need to offer ideas to those who still can't figure out what present to give.

While the "presents" develop their moves, the birthday child can get ready for the party. He or she can get up, dress, brush teeth, polish shoes, set the table, hang the streamers, or blow up the balloons.

Give the children a few minutes to practice and then ask them to spread out around the room and climb into imaginary boxes.

The birthday child selects a present, carefully unties the "box," unwraps the gift paper and takes the top off. Out comes the present, doing its thing. When the present finishes moving (either around the room or in a small area, depending on the nature of the present), it climbs back into its box, and the birthday child gets a chance to guess what the present was. If he or she cannot guess, let the other children try. If no one can guess, ask the present to perform again, perhaps with a hint or two about how to make the movements clearer, and allow the birthday child three questions to help identify the gift.

Once through is enough for this game. If you are working with more than twelve children, let them pick partners and both become part of the same present—in the same "box." If they choose to give a bicycle as a present, each child can be one of the wheels. If they choose a Polaroid camera, one child can be the camera, complete with shutter that clicks, and the other the picture that pops out. If they select a badminton set, one can be the racket and the other, the shuttlecock. And so on.

Christmas or Chanuka special:

Ask the children to work out movements for the presents they would like to get!

MOVEMENT TAG

Tag with a twist.

This is an update of one of the world's oldest games. Choose one child to be "It." He or she stands in the middle of the room. The rest of the group divides in two: one group in a line against one wall, the other group against the opposite wall. "It" yells out a movement command such as "Skip!" All the children must now "skip" to the opposite wall without being tagged by "It." "It" must also skip as he tries to tag those attempting to cross. A "tag" is a touch only; anyone who hits, punches or tackles is O-U-T and joins you on the sidelines. As soon as "It" tags someone, that child takes the middle position as "It," while everyone scrambles to safety against the walls. "It" issues a new command, such as "Hop and turn," and the game continues.

If the "It" child is having trouble tagging someone, and hasn't succeeded after a reasonable length of time, choose another "It," perhaps let one of your tacklers back into the game.

If space is limited you might confine "Its" domain to a 2- or 3-foot strip down the middle of the room parallel to the safety walls. The easiest way to mark off this strip is with two pieces of masking tape. Then the strip becomes the only danger zone the children have to pass, though they must skip or jump or gallop their entire time on the floor. The only time they may relax is when they touch one of the two safety walls.

As umpire, make sure no one waits too long by the wall to avoid getting caught. You can penalize wallflowers by making them the new "It" or asking them to join you on the sidelines, since they're not really playing the game.

Encourage the children to choose unusual word commands, after they have gone through the usual list of run, gallop, turn, jump, hop, skip. Try things like skate, slide, crawl, limp, lunge, walk knock-kneed or bow-legged. These add spice and novelty and can be hilarious.

RIDICULOUS CHARADES

No signs or symbols in these *charades.*

Write the descriptions of characters and situations on slips of paper, fold them, and put them in a box or bag. In these two-person charades, children select partners and each pair chooses one piece of paper which contains the information for their charade.

Point out that talking is not allowed, and that the group can only guess who they are and what they are doing by the way they do it. We can tell a bullfighter, for example, by the sweeping motions of his cape and his small deft steps. We can tell a bull by his heavy rushing movements.

Send the partners to separate corners, or to find private places in the room for them to work out their movements. While they practice and plan, walk around to each group and see if you can make suggestions or give them ideas for clearer, more dramatic actions.

Choose easier charades for younger children, such as:

1. Dog chases mailman.
2. Shoe salesman tries to please impossible customer.
3. Two kittens play with a ball of yarn.
4. A game of table tennis.
5. Two dancing figures in a music box.
6. Spider catches a fly.

Try more complicated, demanding ideas with older children:

7. Two fuzz balls under a chair in a strong wind.
8. A policeman chases a burglar.
9. Two nearsighted people search for lost contact lenses.
10. A computer meets a robot.
11. Two cowards play sport karate (no touching).
12. Frankenstein meets Dracula.

Ask the children to show that they are ready by sitting near you. If any of them needs a little more time, give it. When everyone is ready, let the first pair perform their charade for the group. When they finish, ask the children to raise their hands if they think they know who the children were and what they were doing. The performers call on them. If the audience has trouble guessing what was going on, let the group know who they were, and ask them for ideas on how to make the charade clearer. After each charade, discuss it with the group: ask them what was good about it, ask them to suggest ways to improve it. If your approach is positive and helpful, the children will be full of ideas. The performers can then repeat the charade, applying the new ideas.

Next time you play, ask the children to think up characters and situations and write them on slips of paper, as many as they want. Use the best of them in your box. If the children pull out their own charade ideas, they can put them back and pick again.

3. DO AS I DO

TAKE ME TO YOUR LEADER

How to watch, invent, and the pleasure of seeing everyone else doing your thing!

This is an excellent game to play with children as young as five years old: it makes them think, define their movements, focus on someone else's movements, analyze them, and translate them into their own bodies.

Start by teaching the movement that says "Come on!" and practice it all together. Put one foot in front of the other, bend your knees, and reach one arm out down low, and continue lifting it outstretched until it circles forward and up, and ends close to your face.

When everyone knows the arm motion, add the body movement: bend forward, and let your body follow your arm as it circles forward and up, actually continuing your arm's circle. Finish with your arm close to your body and lean back. If you ask the children what the movement means, they'll know at once that you are saying "Come on," and they enjoy the clear direct translation. Perhaps at this point you might discuss with the group the fact that movement is an international language; that once you say it in movement, you don't need any further explanation in words. We can watch American Indian rain dances, African voodoo ceremonies, or Indian mudras, and we know what they are saying. No translators needed!

When everyone can say "Come on" in movement, start the game. Explain that each child will have a turn being the Leader and may select any means to get across the floor. Give them time to decide on the movement they want: walking, skipping, sliding, running, turning, hopping, crawling—whatever.

Assemble the group in one corner of the room, and choose your first Leader. Stand behind that child, hold his shoulders, and point him toward the diagonally opposite corner. Tell him to use whatever movement he has chosen to get into that corner, starting now. When the child arrives at the opposite corner, he turns to the group, puts one foot in front of the other, and calls them with his arm.

Don't let the rest of the children start off immediately. First define the movement verbally, pointing out the kind of a movement it is, where the Leader's hands were, whether he lifted his knees up in the front or out to the side. When you talk about the Leader's movements and define them, it makes the children more alert, more aware of the different parts of the body and their possibilities, more analytical about their own movements. They begin to see more sharply and clearly.

When the children are in the right starting position, at your signal, they cross the room to the Leader, repeating the same movement he used. Then choose another Leader, but point him or her toward the directly opposite corner, and repeat the process. Point the third Leader toward the diagonally opposite corner so that eventually you use all four corners of the room and are ready to start the pattern again. The shape for this is:

START

If the Leader selects a complex movement pattern, ask him to repeat it so it becomes clear to the other children. Sometimes the children get carried away, and change the movement many times as they cross the floor. Don't let them get away with it. It must be a clear movement that can be repeated by the group.

40

You might want to use a rhythm instrument to accompany the movements. Sometimes the children are reluctant to move until they hear an accompanying sound—a piano chord, a drum beat, or just a clap—and any sound will get them started. As you watch the movement, you can adapt your rhythm to theirs.

Sometimes the children are so happy to make it to the other side, they completely forget to call their friends to follow them; there is dead silence and nothing happens. Instead of telling the Leader to call the group, ask why they aren't coming. The Leader will catch on, smile, and call them.

Encourage the children to be inventive and try new ways of moving, rather than repeating the same old skipping and galloping. If shy children select patterns that have already been done, sometimes it is wise to ignore the repetition, but generally push them toward trying something new, even if you have to whisper a few ideas. With older children suggest that they make a movement combination out of two different steps, such as a skip and a turn, a hop and a jump.

When each child has had a chance to be the Leader, and the group has used all the basic locomotor patterns, ask the children for more ideas of how to get across the floor. Suggest a theme, such as tricks an acrobat might do, and they will come up with somersaults, fancy rolls, and cartwheels. The next time you play the game ask them to be different animals as they cross the floor: a snake wiggling on its belly, a bird flying, a kangaroo hopping, a frog jumping. They can be means of transportation: one will be a train, others cars, busses, planes, ocean liners, motorcycles, sailboats. Ask the group to guess what the Leader is after he or she moves across the floor.

THE MIRROR GAME

Requires a great deal of concentration, but it's worth it.

The children choose partners, and line up facing them. One line is the "mirror player"; the other the "mirror image."

Talk about actually looking into your mirror at home, and seeing the "mirror image." When you lift your left hand, the mirror image lifts its right hand at exactly the same time. That immediate response is what we want to achieve in this game.

Start off counting aloud. At each count, the mirror player makes a move, and the mirror image does the same thing, just a split second later. At the beginning, the children should use only one part of their bodies. Let them sit, face each other, and use only their heads. Ask the mirror players to explore all the possibilities of movement. Now ask them to use only their shoulders, then only their fingers. At this point, let them add their wrists; after that add their elbows, so that they are using their arms completely.

When you have explored each part in movement, tell the children they are free to do whatever they choose. Give them only one restriction: the position you want them to work in—sitting, kneeling, standing in one spot, or moving through space. It is a good idea to work in that order, which allows more and more freedom as it flows from small to large movement. Of course, the children must change parts, so that each has a turn to be the mirror player and the mirror image.

It takes a great deal of concentration to watch and imitate precisely, so don't let this game go on too long before changing parts. It is an excellent way to develop perception and focus and it leads the children to new and more inventive ways of moving.

THE MAD PUPPETEER

Mis-strung marionettes and new discoveries in balance.

Unless we are acrobats or mountain-climbers, dancers or athletes, we usually take balance for granted. In this improvisation, the "puppets" suddenly realize that they can balance from many different points. As a result of each crooked stringing, they must find a new "center" in their own bodies. It is a fresh concept for most children and a very challenging one.

Premise: A puppeteer works on an assembly line stringing newly-made marionettes. The job gets so monotonous that one day he goes mad and decides to re-string the puppets his own way.

Tell the children to spread themselves out around the room and lie in a heap on the floor: they are newly-made marionettes. You are the Mad Puppeteer. Choose a body part that you will string the puppets by. Call out, for example, "Chin." Then count aloud as you beat six times on a drum, or pot, or just clap. During the six counts, the puppets rise to a full standing position, but their chins must lead them because the string is attached to their chins and is pulling on them. After the six counts, drop the strings and the puppets collapse to the floor. Now you are ready to call out a different body part and start again.

Experiment with the idea of the string connections. Get the children to try rising as though the string was coming from the middle of their backs. How would they get up if a string was pulling on their toes or heels? What if it was attached to one knee? Or to a nose?

Remind the puppets that the part the string pulls must stretch to its utmost, while the rest of the body hangs back.

Now, as the Mad Puppeteer, stand in the middle of the room. Stretch your arms out in front of you, as if you are holding the bar where the strings are tied. When you hold the puppets' strings, you control their movements. In "puppet language" it is time for the marionettes to go to school, which means they will learn to walk and move, bow and turn, gesture and swing— as the Mad Puppeteer dictates.

Let us say that you have just strung the marionettes from their elbows and given them the six-count to rise:

1. Jerk the imaginary "bar" in the air a few times. The puppets will need to jump up and down leading with their elbows, reaching and stretching them as high as they can.

2. Still holding the invisible bar, run once around the room. The puppets must follow, bodies hanging back, elbows leading in a sideways drag.

3. Still holding the bar, spin around in place. The puppets must do the same, again pulled by the elbow which leads them.

There are many other possibilities. With the puppets watching you closely, you can seesaw the bar from side-to-side, wiggle it, plunge it suddenly, and the puppets must respond—elbows first!

Lower the bar gently, and the puppets crumple to the floor. Call out a new body part. In six counts, raise the strings, and the puppets are ready to repeat the sequence.

The next time you play, let the children take turns being the Mad Puppeteer. Encourage them to find new ways to move the puppets. Just make sure that all eyes focus on the Mad Puppeteer at all times, and that the movement directions are clear.

SCULPTOR AND CLAY

A time-tested game that adds a new dimension—responsibility for another person.

A popular game for all children is "Molding," or "Sculptor and Clay." Divide the group into partners; it's a good idea to pair off the children fairly equally in terms of weight. One child is the Sculptor and the other the Clay. They will switch roles in the middle.

"Sculptor" tells "Clay" in which position to start; Clay can stand, sit, kneel, lie, or curl up in a ball. Then Sculptor picks up Clay's arm, let's say, and moves it around until the position pleases him, perhaps with Clay's arm straight up in the air and the hand dangling down. Clay has no will of its own and must stay the way it is put, allowing the Sculptor to make all the decisions. Sculptor might balance the Clay on one leg, bend it forward or turn its head from left to right until it hits the "right" angle. In each case, Clay should be as relaxed as possible while Sculptor molds it and then should try to hold the final position.

This game requires some judgment on Sculptor's part. Hopefully, he or she doesn't try to lift both of Clay's feet in the air at the same time. When the children have the responsibility for another person's shape and balance, however, you'll find that they grow more considerate and aware of the human body. Don't worry about the tumbles (there will be a few). Clay has naturally self-protective instincts and won't remain in too uncomfortable a position and, of course, the Sculptor knows his turn will come.

When each child has had a turn being both Clay and Sculptor, take this game into movement. Instead of molding still positions, Sculptor lifts an arm and spins Clay around. Whatever position Clay ends up in, there it stays. Sculptor may sway Clay from side to side, lift its foot and make it hop. Each action should travel (even if only a sway in place) and continue for about ten seconds. If you are working with a large group, let half of it watch while the other half works, so there is plenty of room.

After the group gets used to sculpting and being sculpted, let them pair off themselves. Now you can begin to develop a sense of phrasing (flow) and cohesiveness. Sculptor finds five or so positions for Clay in rapid succession, and after rehearsing them a few times, Clay should be able to go into the positions alone, as if someone was moving it. Then Sculptor's task is to make up different sounds for each position; as he makes a sound, Clay goes into the corresponding position, so that Sculptor "orchestrates" his subject. When Sculptor and Clay can go through these movements and sounds smoothly, they present them to the group.

4. PANTOMIME TRIPS

Before you start on any "trip" it is important to set the scene for it. Talk about it with the group. Chances are wherever you're going someone in the group has already been there and can add important facts about what it was like and what there is to do.

Then choose a means of transportation to get you there and back: it could be by train, plane, motorcycle, tugboat, rocket, tail of a kite, camelback. Start off with mind-trips that could really happen, and then take a trip to an imaginary place, or to a real place the children have never been to (such as the moon). Limit yourself to one trip for each session that the group meets, and the children will eagerly look forward to going to the place of the day.

HOUSE OF GLASS—HOUSE OF FIRE   Ages 4-8

An exciting trip for younger children to magical places.

These two special houses have an element of magic and mystery about them. When you talk to your group, try to get that feeling into your voice.

Ask if they have ever been to a house of glass. Explain that the glass is delicate: the sun shines through it and sparkles and shimmers. Whisper, because the House of Glass is so fragile that if you make a loud noise, it will shatter and break. Explain that as they pass through the House of Glass, they must move very softly and gently, taking running steps on the tips of their toes.

Still whispering, ask them to get on line behind you and lead the line in different directions around the room: in a circle, in a pattern, into corners. Sit down quietly in the House of Glass and ask the children to look around and whisper to you what they see: Does the color of the sunshine change as it passes through the glass? Can they feel the warmth of the sun if they close their eyes? What happens to the walls of glass when it rains?

"Now we are moving out of the House of Glass, through the door of the House of Glass, and Whew, now we can talk in our normal voices and don't have to whisper any more!"

Lead them into another house, a very hot one, one with smoke pouring out of the windows, flames licking the roof. "Now we are in the House of Fire, and we have to skip very high in the air, otherwise, our feet will burn."

Make this a very short trip. It is an intense one, as the children will use all their energy to really skip high, and they will be relieved when you lead them out of the House of Fire. Ask them to sit down on the grass outside and tell what they saw and felt inside. What colors were the flames? Where did the fire go? Could they pull away a piece of fire? Did it come in waves like the ocean? Did it run like a brook?

48

TRIP TO THE BEACH

The best part of the trip is sneaking up on the waves at low tide!

In warm weather, and sometimes in the middle of winter, you might want to go to the beach. Some children can form a train, by lining up and holding the waist of the child in front. Blow the whistle, and the train starts. Other children that live nearer the beach may want to ride imaginary bikes. Anyone on a bike should obey traffic signals, and perhaps one or two children can fill in as traffic cops; hold up their hands for a red light and wave their arms to let the traffic pass. Bikes can move in the middle of the room, while the train circles the outside. Eventually all disembark and land on the beach.

Divide the room in half: one part is the sandy beach, and the other the water. First you can walk along the shore and kick the sand way up with your toes, as high as you can kick. The sand is so inviting that almost everyone will want to make sand castles. (If any child hasn't done this in real life, it's time to learn, even if only in imagination.) To build a castle, scoop out the sand and pat it onto your structure, watch it grow larger and shape it all the while. Some children will be more interested in the scooping-out process, and may want to dig tunnels under the sand. If two children start at opposite ends and dig towards each other, they can join hands eventually under the sand; but at this very special beach they can crawl through their tunnels and wiggle out the other end. Possibilities are endless; the best thing to do is to rely on the children. They will explore it in new ways.

Now everyone picks a partner; one lies flat while the other covers him or her with sand. The standing partner should be sure to cover the toes and fingers and torso and shoulders—every part of the partner, except the head. Make it clear, even when playing, that sand in the eyes is painful and can lead to injury. When the children report that their partners are completely buried in the sand, let them jump up, shake the sand off, and change rôles.

The sun is strong, so it's time to go swimming. Everyone walks down to the water's edge and jumps or dives in. Once in, they can swim, float on their stomachs, do somersaults and tricks in the water, but at a slower tempo

since the water makes it hard to move. When everyone has had enough, it's time to run out, wrap up in big beach towels, and rub every part of their bodies dry—faces, too.

Lunchtime—from bag lunches. Ask each child "What kind of sandwich did your parents pack?" Each will delight in telling you. After their apples or cookies, wrap up the garbage and very deliberately go to an imaginary garbage pail in the corner and throw it in.

You can't go swimming right after lunch and you can discuss why not: how you can get cramps easily and that is why it is important to wait half-an-hour or an hour before going into the water. Let them rest for a few moments before going down to the shore. It's low tide now and the children can tiptoe out where the water used to be in an effort to sneak up on the tide and CRASH!—either strike a loud chord on the piano or bang on a drum, and let the sound of the approaching tide send them scurrying back to the shore so they don't get wet.

"Did you get wet?" you can ask (perhaps one or two weren't quick enough).

Try it once more. The joy is in not knowing when the CRASH is going to come; if everyone screams, don't be alarmed—it's an elated fear. Two low tides should happily wear out the children, without wearing out the fun and novelty of the game.

Time to go home. Those who came by train can reassemble and chug back; those with bicycles can hop on and ride back, perhaps with two different cops. Everyone (you, too) should be ready for a good rest.

TRIP TO THE FARM

Especially satisfying for city kids who don't often get a chance to visit a farm.

It's good to talk about the trip a little, at the beginning, especially if you're working with city kids. Start by discussing farm animals, the foods we get from them, and farm chores, but keep the talking minimal. You might want to save most of it for the end so that they can tell about their experiences visiting or living on a farm while they rest.

Let the children pick out their own name for the farm (Old MacDonald's, Gilligan's Farm, etc.). On this trip, you can go by pony. To mount, put one leg high over the pony's back, then gallop around the room in the direction of the farm. After circling the room three times, you arrive at the farm. Dismount and tie up at the post.

First stop is the chicken house. Let half or three-quarters of the children be clucking chickens, while the rest clutch baskets of feed, and bending low, throw handfuls to the eager chickens who gobble it up. Throw feed in the other direction so that all the chickens are fed. You might want to switch halfway so that everyone has a turn feeding and being fed. Watch what starts to happen naturally, and encourage the children to carry it out all the way. If the chickens get so hungry and greedy, for example, that they surround the feeder and start pecking, the feeder might drop the whole basket, and run away, giving the chickens a field day.

Next stop is the cowshed. Let the children pick names for the cows they plan to milk, take imaginary three-legged stools and milk pails from the corner and sit on them right beside the invisible cows. With one hand after the other, pull on the udders to get the milk out efficiently. As each pail fills, the milker takes it (with great care, because it is full and heavy) to a big, imaginary storage bin in the corner where the milk is collected. When the children finish milking—as many cans as they want—they return their pails and stools to the corner.

Out of the cowshed and into the sunny fields lined with berries—raspberries and blackberries. Let the children pick as many as they can, dodging thorns, climbing over and under vines, ducking the over-hanging branches.

Pick a large bag full. Who can pick the most berries? Put your berry bag in the pack on your pony's back.

Now for the most fun of the trip. Carefully climb up the steep ladder (one hand over the other) that leads to the hayloft. Start by throwing hay at each other, and then tumble in the hay, and roll in it. Here's a chance to try all kinds of tricks, because the hay is soft. You can do cartwheels, headstands and walk on your hands. After a good frolic and before things get too wild, it's time to go home. Climb down and unhitch the ponies. Mount, get comfortable in the saddle, decide whom you will bring berries home to (perhaps Grandma could make some jam) and ride off into the sunset.

20,000 LEAGUES

Trip to a slow-motion world.

Your group is going on a pioneer journey underneath the sea. Since you need a vessel to get there, have the children line up to form a submarine: the first two children raise their arms as the periscope; it might help to explain that the periscope is the "eye" of the ship. First the submarine must submerge (get lower and lower as it travels around the room). The periscope people lead the group, wave their hands slowly when it isn't safe to go, and hold the group back until the danger is past.

When the submarine is totally submerged (the group crouched as low as possible), let the group slowly disperse. Explain that they are under water and, in water, their bodies are lighter. They must move slowly because of the resistance of the water; there can be no sudden actions; sometimes they can float. Let them move as you talk.

On the next step in the journey they become seaweed. Since it is very light, and has no will or weight of its own, the waves may push seaweed into all sorts of strange entangled twistings. You might want to use music at this point; perhaps a recording of some airy flute or "watery" music, and encourage the children to roll on the floor, against a wall, to tangle their bodies in interesting and unusual ways and shapes.

Two pieces of seaweed could become entangled with each other and change their shapes as the water pushes them in different directions and toward and away from each other. To accelerate the movement, you can make the music louder. If you have no recorded music, you can shake a tambourine or pair of maracas for effect.

When the seaweed untangles, the group becomes sea turtles. They go onto their knees and lean on their forearms. Once they are crouched in this position, explain that a sea turtle moves by advancing its right arm and foot at the same time, then its left arm and foot. This produces a waddling effect, just the opposite of our right-arm-left-leg style of walking, and it is an unusual co-ordination which produces a strange sensation. Once in a while, the turtle reaches its long neck out, searching for food—or has it heard something? Let the children experiment with reaching their necks out as far as they will go.

Add to the story; give a loud bang on a pot or drum, even yell a loud sound from time to time. That frightens the turtles, so they hurriedly draw their necks and heads in and hide them deep within themselves. Elements of surprise are always welcome: improvise, make up variations and add as you go along.

One or more children can become a Portuguese man o'war. You might show them a picture of a real man o'war jellyfish, explain how dangerous they are, and that they're never to be touched. These creatures are soft and slinky; they slowly undulate their arms and legs, hoping to engulf anything that comes their way. Other children can be tiny fish that float on their bellies, trying to escape the clutches of the men o'war. If a fish is caught, he must roll over "wounded" to the side of the room, for the soft blobs are powerful and poisonous.

When most of the fish are caught (or after a few minutes), tell the children to relax on the floor with their arms stretched over their heads. They are now ordinary jellyfish. This is one of the most delightful parts of the game, but it calls for great concentration from you. Walk over to a child and ask, "Are you as relaxed as a jellyfish would be?"

Lift his or her other arm or leg and see if it's very heavy; it should be if the weight of the body is entrusted to you. Explain that when someone is totally relaxed and you pick up his or her arm, it should feel very heavy and go down with a thud when you release it. If the children are relaxed, give them each a "ride." Pull each one around in circles by that arm or leg, turning, spinning, or spiraling them across the floor. If you don't have enough space, only do this with a few children. Give the rest a turn next time. When you finish with the "rides," throw their leg or arm over them in any position and explain that they must freeze that way.

It is time now to come back from the bottom of the sea. Reassemble the submarine. The ship rises, until the periscope is above the water line. Everyone emerges when the boat docks and is glad to feel dry land.

OTHER TRIPS

There are many more trips you and your group can take. How about a trip to the moon? Climb into your spacesuit, get ready for the countdown, and then blast off into space—with feelings of weightlessness. You can explore the moon's surface, and collect samples of rocks to bring back to earth. You can also take photographs of strange things that you find.

How about a trip to a Robot Repair Factory where all the robot parts have to be taken off, oiled, cleaned and screwed back in again!

On a trip to the circus, you can be a tightrope walker, an acrobat, a fat lady, a giant, a juggler and many more. Most of the children will have been to a circus, and will have dozens of ideas.

How about a trip back through time? Take rowboats (one for each traveller) sit on the floor and really pull on those oars. You might go all the way back to the cavemen. You can hunt, fish, prepare food, hide from dinosaurs.

Try a mountain-climbing expedition: think of all the things you will need to pack and carry with you, and all the different ways of climbing—be sure to use a rope and drive spikes into the rocks, on at least part of your trip.

Want more places to go? Ask the kids.

5. GROUP IMPROVISATIONS

THE MARVELOUS MACHINE

Where people are parts—a high note for any meeting or party.

Tell the children they're going to construct a huge machine and they themselves will be the parts. Each part must have its own sound, and each part must touch (with some parts of its body) another person-machine-part; otherwise there are no limitations on the type, shape or sound the machine part may have.

Ask the children about machines they have seen in operation. They surely have seen clocks, phonographs, escalators, typewriters, and sewing machines, and they may have seen bottling plants, car-wash stations, computers, switchboards, postage meters, blenders, motors, gears, smoke stacks, sanitation trucks, cranes, dump trucks, and cement mixers. Talk about the moving parts of the machines they know: what they do, how they move, how the parts relate to each other, how they attach and what sounds they make. Point out that each moving part produces the same movement and sound over and over again.

For example, take the typewriter. The obvious parts that move are the keys, the roller, and the ribbon. Experiment with the hammer-action keys. Suggest that the children lie on their backs with bent arms and legs; each time you create a clicking sound with your tongue, a leg or an arm will stretch up, hit the imaginary paper and return to its original position. Only one key can work at a time, but two keys might get stuck together!

Experiment with the roller: you would inch slowly across the room, ring a bell, slam back, move to the next line and start again.

As the ribbon, you are wound around a spool. You would move continuously with very small motions while the keys are striking, jump up when someone strikes a capital letter, and stop when the typing stops. Then you would wind yourself around the other spool and start back again.

Analyze other machines the same way. The children will grasp the essence of the mechanical movement quickly and begin to create their own contraptions.

The machine that you are going to build together will be a supermachine. Before you start, ask the children what its function will be. They will always come up with original imaginative ideas.

Start with one child, who comes to the middle of the room and begins a machine-like motion with an accompanying sound. Try to pick an inventive, outgoing child so the machine starts off with a flourish. When the child is going strong (about twenty seconds should do it), the second child, who is waiting in line along the wall or in a corner, attaches to the first one by a hand, a foot, an elbow, a hip—whatever—and begins his or her own different and unique movement and sound. The third person has a choice of attaching to either the first or second child, so the machine can end in a spiral or a cluster or simply in chaos, which is fun, too.

Make sure that you can hear each sound, and emphasize the importance of the children's retaining their own movements and sounds. It is only too easy to adjust to the dominant rhythm pattern. If you can maintain syncopation and counter-rhythms, so much the better.

When everyone is participating, call above the noise, "I'm going to slow the machine down, so it should get slower a-n-d- s-l-o-w-e-r. . ." Slow them with your voice; keep talking, as the sound and action becomes lower and creakier, and finally coax it to a halt.

Then immediately: "I'm winding the machine up. It's getting faster-and-faster!" and talk them back into full action and noise. Accelerate not only motions but the accompanying sounds, and talk them into faster rhythms. Walk around the machine as you spur them on until the children barely have time to complete their movements and are shouting their sounds. You will have a wild invention that usually ends in a machine breakdown and much laughter.

The group develops a splendid feeling of "oneness" when they construct and work this machine, and the glow lasts a long time.

MODERN TIMES

This electrical nightmare makes us take a fresh look at the world around us.

If we don't have modern kitchens ourselves, almost all of us have seen them on television, so everyone will know what you mean when you tell them they're going to become household appliances.

Divide the children into groups of three (you can vary the number, but it is easier to work with threes). Each group must turn itself into an electrical appliance: a vacuum cleaner, toaster, can opener, washing machine, or power saw with its accompanying sound.

It's a good idea to precede the improvisation with a discussion of appliances and their moving parts. Take the electric blender: it has rotating blades that can move at different speeds, depending upon which button you press. The unit of three could break down into two blades and one piece of bread, or one blade and two carrots. The children may put anything they want in the blender, but once the blades start turning, the food, whatever it is, must jump between them, as it is chopped to bits. The garbage disposal works in much the same way with horrendous noises.

Take the washing machine: (1) It has an agitator which twists, spins and stops. It needs (2) soap and water and (3) dirty clothes. Suggest that the children go through a complete (but shortened) wash, rinse, and spin cycle. For a dishwasher: substitute dirty dishes and silver for clothes. Point out that when the dishes are dry, they will be hot and shining, quite different from the soiled, greasy, sticky dishes that went in.

A freezer: Try creating an ice-cube tray, filled with water, each cube must firm, stiffen and crystallize into solid ice.

A broiler: Prepare two lamb chops on a pan. The flames reach down from above and brush over the chops, which sizzle, flame up, and might even catch on fire.

An electric beater: Parts are the rotating beaters, and add the batter that you choose. You can whip cream, beat egg whites into a stiff froth, churn butter, or cream chocolate sauce. Mashed potatoes are the most fun.

When the children are machine parts, encourage them to use their joints—wrists, elbows, shoulders, hips, knees, ankles in angular bend-and-stretch or rotating motions.

Give them five or ten minutes to work out their presentations. At the end of that time all the groups come together from their respective corners and sit, while one-by-one each unit performs. The audience must guess the correct appliance; it's not always so easy. An over-enthusiastic piece of toast might jump up and down unremittingly in response to a fellow toaster; and a pitiful piece of dust could be sucked in, time and time again, by a relentless, two-headed vacuum cleaner. Be sure, in a game like this, that the children have a chance to change rôles.

If you want to take this further, when a group has an appliance that interests them, they can make up a story about it. A typewriter key can get separated from its brothers and sisters; a housewife can be swept into her vacuum cleaner and become "Alice in Vacuumland," a precious painting can fall into the washing machine. Let the children's imagination run wild. Absurd situations are a good change and help us look at familiar objects in a new light.

THE ELEVATOR

A simple experiment in mime.   **Ages 7-up**

The elevator or lift lends itself especially well to improvisations. All sorts of comic and dramatic events can take place as it ups and downs or doesn't. Divide the group into small units—four, five, or six children, and ask each unit to work out a dramatic situation.

The scene can be anything from an apartment house or department store to a hospital. Two children form the sliding door of the elevator. They may stand side by side, step apart to open, and—"ZUT"—snap together. They may stand face to face, elbows bent and palms touching, and open by stepping backwards and dropping their arms abruptly. When the elevator moves, they make a zooming-up or -down sound to indicate motion.

When the elevator goes up, all passengers go up on their toes. When the elevator goes down, they go down, too, on their knees. Passengers get off and on, find themselves on the wrong floors, go up when they want to go down. The elevator doors, of course, have a mind of their own. They may refuse to let some people out. They may catch slow passengers between them. They may prefer to go down when everyone pressed "Up" (this is easy to mime, and children are naturals at it), or stop between floors. Passengers can bang on the walls, remove the top of the elevator, even climb the cable to the next floor.

Encourage the children to exaggerate everyday movement. Talking, for example, should involve fingers, arms, and shoulders, as well as head and neck, and *must be soundless*. The only sounds come from the elevator doors, and whenever they make them, passengers must go up on their toes or down on their knees, whatever else they're doing.

Ask the group to think up dramatic situations of their own: a team of scientists who have captured a Blob from outer space might try to get the thing analyzed in the laboratory on a different floor. This leads inevitably to struggles with the growing Blob, strange transformations, stuck elevators and mad scientists.

If several groups are working, try putting them all together in a huge building with many elevators. The president of a bank, for example, who must transfer money to a secret vault, may be waylaid by a bunch of thieves, and try to escape by darting from elevator to elevator (some of them on his or her side, and some against). Then people not only get in and out at different floors, but they can switch into different cars, too.

A monkey might get away from its owner, steal hats, purses, and packages and slip from one car to another with its owner in hot pursuit. In matters of plot lines, you may safely leave it to the kids, who, depending upon their backgrounds and life styles, will come up with a broad range of pertinent situations.

When you deal with large involved improvisations, such as these, always start with a simple premise and work your way into the drama. This way, the group will feel a sense of continuity and see that all things stem from a source. This concept will carry over into other creative areas, as the children grow accustomed to starting with a small idea when they want to construct a more complex painting, song, story or sculpture.

THE AWFUL ORCHESTRA

Ages 8-up

An unbeatable introduction to the instruments of the orchestra and much more—this improvisation is also wonderful fun.

This rewarding improvisation can be as simple or as complex as you choose to make it. You can perform it in half an hour or extend it to a long-range project.

As a complex program, you need more preparation than you do for any of the other games, but it becomes a memorable experience for everyone in the group.

First you need to collect photographs of the musical instruments that make up an orchestra, and pictures of musicians actually playing them. You can find pictures galore in children's books about musical instruments. You will also need a tape recorder and a tape which you can prepare ahead of time.

If you are going to work with an entire orchestra, begin the tape with a symphony—Beethoven works well; so does Brahms. After a minute or so, stop the tape and very abruptly change to jazz music, boogie woogie, or rock. Let that continue for about thirty seconds, and then return to the classical piece you started with. Repeat the sequence. You will use the tape much later when the group is ready to "perform."

If you would rather work quickly with small groups and fewer instruments, substitute chamber music, and create several string quartets, each with its own conductor. Try Mozart and Bach for selections.

Start out by discussing with the children the many instruments that make up an orchestra, or just the string instruments for the short version. Bring out the photographs you have selected and talk about each instrument individually. If you have any recordings of the instrument in solo performance, so much the better.

Find out if any of the children in the group play any of the instruments. Ask them to bring them in and explain their workings. Then, when everyone has seen and studied an instrument, ask the children to make believe they are holding it and playing it.

Violin: Hold it with your left arm in front of you, elbow bent, and wrist twisted to the right so your fingers can rest on the strings. Grip it with your shoulder and tuck it against your cheek. The right arm holds the bow. Keep your bowing arm loose as it sweeps back and forth across the strings.

Cello: To play your imaginary cello, sit with legs spread apart so the cello can rest on the floor. Your left hand can start at shoulder level as you press the strings to make the notes lower or higher. Your right arm holds the bow and glides back and forth at the center of the cello.

Double Bass: When you mind-play this giant, your arm positions will be the same as they are for the cello.

Harp: Sit with the top of the harp over your right shoulder. Pluck the strings from each side, left arm on left side of the harp. Tilt the instrument toward you as you play. Press the pedals (there are seven of them) to change pitch.

THE STRINGS

Take the time to get the feel of each instrument, of its size, shape and tone quality, so that everyone is at home with the instrument and familiar with it.

Now discuss the word "distortion" and how it applies to movement. Talk about the mirrors in a fun house, and let the children experiment with the effects they create. Then take the actual movement of the musician and *distort* it: start with a basic motion and elongate it, enlarge it, shrink it, so that everyone can see that the "distorted" movement is merely an extension of the original movement, which develops a life of its own.

Our violinists will stand. Their bowing arms move back and forth, can go farther and farther in each direction until they lead into a sidewards hop; extend them still farther and they might even spin into a turn. The other arm which holds the violin can move upward until it points to the sky or down to the floor. These are just a few of the possibilities. As the children work on their own distortions, they will invent their own movements. If you see an unusual distortion, point it out to the group.

Cello: Since the musician is sitting on a chair and can balance on it, he or she is free to extend one or both legs high in the air as the bowing arm sweeps back and forth in as long a line as possible. The cellist can balance at the edge of the seat with head uplifted and lean way back; his or her fingers can jump in an arc onto different spots on the keyboard.

The double bass player has almost no movement limitations. Legs, feet and hips are free to move in place and in space. The musician is rooted only by the double bass itself, but he or she can go around it or beside it and move it all the way front or back. The bowing arm can move in the same distorted motions as the violin or cello.

Harp: The harpist can move the instrument front and back at extreme angles, can pluck the strings intensely, swooping an arm down or shooting it up in a total stretch. The harpist's feet can stomp on the pedals, press them with heels only, or tickle them with toes.

The feet of all string musicians can tap in time to the rhythm or against it; they can shuffle, criss-cross or create any pattern on the floor.

70

If you want to work with a complete orchestra, you would work now with the woodwind section.

WOODWINDS

Flute: It is held to the side and you *blow across* the mouthpiece instead of into it. The flutist's body is free to move in any distorted way. The hands holding the flute can move from side to side, up or down or in a circle.

The oboe and clarinet are about the same length as the flute, but held to the front. You can use the same movements when you distort them. The oboe-clarinet movement can rock your body, so that you lean forward and back, your knees bend lower and lower until they reach the floor—then they push you into a jump. You can swing sidewards, shake your hips, knock your knees, move anywhere on the floor. The instrument itself can move in any direction.

The bassoon is much longer than the clarinet or the oboe. Sit when you play it. Hold it across your body at an angle, resting the lower part against your hip. If you have a bassoon player in your group, he or she can demonstrate the playing movements, but the bassoon doesn't lend itself easily to complex distortion.

BRASS

When you play any brass instrument, you squeeze your lips together to force out a stream of air between them. The tighter your lips, the harder you must blow.

Trumpet: Press down on the valves to change the notes and hold the trumpet up in front of you. When you distort the movements, your body is completely free to dip, curve, swing, spiral, wiggle, bend and move in space. You can move the trumpet in any direction as you can the flute, clarinet or oboe.

The slide trombone is the most interesting in the brass section for movement possibilities. Instead of pushing down valves as with the trumpet, you change the note by pulling the slide in and out. Movements are entirely free, as they are for the trumpet, except that you have the extra advantage of extending the slide, for good strong stretches.

The French horn and tuba are more limited in their distortion possibilities, so unless a child in the group plays one of them, it is better to concentrate on the other brass instruments.

PERCUSSION

Timpani: These are the kettle drums. Surround the musician on three sides with three invisible drums which he or she plays with two sticks, switching from one drum to the next. Anything goes, as long as the player stays in the vicinity of the drums—even getting down on the floor and reaching up, even turning and playing them behind your back—even dancing while you play.

Cymbals: Strike them together, one moving up while the other moves down. Play them high, play them low, play them turning, moving in space, even while lying on the floor.

Tambourine: Shake it like a bell or bang it like a drum or both. Your body can extend the shaking movement, and you can move in space in any direction.

Triangle: Hold it loosely and tap the outside with an imaginary metal stick, or slip the stick inside the apex of the triangle and trill it quickly back and forth. Your body can extend the trilling movement and you can move freely in space.

Xylophone: Two rows of keys in front of you like a short piano keyboard, and you hit them with two sticks. Use the same sort of movement that you'd use for the kettle drums, but you must be more delicate, because you have to hit the exact imaginary key.

The saxophone, the piano, the guitar and the recorder, while children in the group may play them, are not included in a standard orchestra and are used for special effects and in special pieces.

Experiment with mind-playing all the instruments with fingers, arms, and mouths in their specific positions. Then let the children select the instruments they want to play and give them a chance to work out their individual distorted movements. Arrange them into separate sections—string, woodwind, brass and percussion. The orchestra will be "awful," because at a signal, it will distort the shape of its movements. The movements will change from even to jerky, from fluid to sharp, unexpected and weird.

Select one child to be the conductor who will lead the orchestra with a real or imaginary baton. If you are using several string quartets, choose a conductor for each one. Then start the tape you prepared ahead of time. At the beginning, let the conductor lead the orchestra in "normal" movements for the symphony or chamber music you chose. At the stop in the tape—and a signal from the conductor—as the music changes to the jazz or rock section, each player (the conductor, too) breaks into "distorted" movements. When the tape stops again, the conductor must pull the group back together and switch to normal, undistorted motion. Make sure all the musicians return to the same relative positions they had at the beginning of the distorted sequence. No matter where they move in space, they must get back in time!

You can experiment with different music and different time segments on the tape, but if you let the distorted sections go on too long, the movements lose precision, get wild and uncontrolled, and your orchestra will fall apart.

Next time you rehearse the Awful Orchestra, ask the children to select different instruments and choose a new conductor.

No one who plays this game will ever again watch an orchestra without a special surge of interest and a feeling of kinship with it.

6. AWARENESS GAMES

BODY BAND

A delightful break—use it when you need a rest.

Sit the group in a large circle and ask the first person to make a sound that the next one will try to repeat. Then that second person thinks of his or her own sound which the next person repeats, and so on around the circle. They can cluck, whistle, wail, whoosh, burp, shout and even use their bodies as instruments: they can snap their fingers, clap, slap their thighs and much more. Lead the group in a chorus of "Jingle Bells," in which the children hum while they create their individual sounds simultaneously.

Once the children explore the sound range of their own bodies, ask them to bring things from home that make interesting sounds, and start your own band. If you bang on pots and pans, you'll make a loud, "homey" noise; you can jiggle a pair of measuring spoons or rub a washboard or beat rhythm on a stool. China plates have their own pure ring: a stick played on a glass filled with water makes an actual musical note. How does a metal scissors sound when you tap it against wood? And how about two butter knives clinked against each other? Or a toothbrush rubbed against your fingers? If anyone has trouble finding a soundmaker at home, lend them a tambourine, drum or maracas, so everyone is set up with an "instrument." If you run short at the last minute, maybe you can find a box of paper clips, two pencils you can tap against each other (like rhythm sticks), a notebook you can hit with a pen, or a spiral pad (you can rub a pencil up and down the wire). In a pinch, you can slap the soles of a pair of shoes together.

Think of a song the whole group knows and can sing along with even without music, like "Clementine" or "Saints Go Marching In." Then with you the conductor, raise your baton and lead your homemade orchestra in its premiere performance.

SENSE GAME

Seeing with your hand and translating mysterious sensations into startling movement.

Touching is one of our first ways of discovering ourselves and the world around us. This game heightens our awareness of the way things feel, sharpens our focus, and forces us to translate our feelings into words and movement. It is exciting to see the children struggle to capture the right words to express exactly what they experienced. Often language fails; and their feelings are so intense that they will invent their own words to describe their sensations. You might want to start a dictionary of new words that the group invents. It will be colorful, explicit, and full of impetus for movement.

Collect an assortment of objects, all with different textures, and hide them well in a shopping bag. Explain to the group that you are going to play a game of "touch" and ask them to line up facing the wall, with their hands cupped behind them. Tell them to keep their eyes closed (they have a tendency to peek); anyone whose eyes are the least bit open will be out of the game and out of the fun.

Then take from your shopping bag a well-sharpened pencil, walk from one child to the next, and as you take each child's hand, jab it lightly with the pencil point. Move quickly, because the children can't hold their eyes closed for very long.

Drop the pencil back in the shopping bag and say, "Okay, open your eyes. Don't tell me what you think I put in your hand. Just tell me what it felt like."

This is an important distinction to make: it starts the children thinking in terms of feelings and sensations. They will answer "Pointy," or "Sharp," or "Hard," but try to get more vivid, evocative words from them. Their perceptions become sharper as they try to express themselves more precisely.

After they explore the feeling of the pencil in words, ask them to move in a "Pointy," or "Sharp," or "Hard" way. By this time they are focused

on the "sharp" sensation and translate it into their bodies as they never could if you showed them the object first. Once they know what the object is, their movements become stereotyped: they react as they think they should. Beat a drum or pot, the wall or floor or any percussive instrument as you say their own words back to them—"A-a-and *Sharp*! —A-a-and *Hard*—A-a-and *Pointy*!—" and so on. Hold each adjective for a few seconds while the children hold the positions they have struck. After they express their feelings in movement, show them the prop you used. They will all say, "I knew it all the time!" or "I knew it was a pencil point!"

Now have them face you at the wall, with open eyes, again touch the pencil point to their hands, and ask if it feels any different now that they know what it is. Chances are they will say "Yes." Ask then to repeat the movement again now. Keep shouting out the words "Sharp" and "Pointy" and the other descriptive words, because the children tend to lose these qualities once they see the object.

Continue the game with other objects, with the children facing the wall, eyes closed, hands cupped behind them.

Try it with a hard boiled egg (smooth, cold), a feather duster (light, airy), a whisk or an egg beater (twirly, hard), sandpaper, a marble, a chain, a wet sponge. Look in your kitchen drawer and in your wastebasket for articles with interesting shapes and textures. Ask the children to bring in things they find that they think will stump the group. Have them wrap their objects well in paper, so that no one will know they are pine cones, rocks, or feathers. Let the child who brings in the object go along the line and touch it to each child's hand.

Other things to replenish your shopping bag? Try a fork, a rubber ball, a jack, a spatula, a shell, a paint brush, a piece of velvet, a pebble.

SOUND MAGIC

You hear more when you listen with your body.

Ask the children to lie on the floor with eyes shut. In this game they will listen to the sound of the instrument and respond to it with movement. Begin with a delicate sound, such as the tinkle of a bell, and explain that they must move to the "music" and stop when the sound stops. The bell sound is light; it shakes, it wiggles. Ask the children to describe it with their bodies —the way they hear it. They can use just wrist and fingers, just ankles and toes, just hips, or their entire bodies. The important thing is to capture the quality of the bell. Start gently: give them periods of silence between the sounds, and then increase pace and volume so that you really have them moving by the end of the bell segment.

If you are lucky enough to get your hands on a large gong, or cymbals, ask the children to close their eyes and listen as you give one loud bang on it, then lift their arms when the sound stops. The overtones of the gong continue for a long time, but some children will raise their hands almost immediately. Say, "I can still hear it," and they will put their hands down and listen more concentratedly. After a few repetitions, you will find that the children hear more and longer, and won't lift a finger until the sound has really disappeared.

Try to get a string of Indian bells—each bell has a different tone. Use them singly or together. See if the children can tell which bell has the highest sound (it is the smallest bell).

Use wooden sticks, a wood or tone block, a recorder, castanets, a triangle, finger cymbals, maracas, a horn, a bamboo flute. Any instrument with a resonant sound will elicit movement.

It is important for the children to keep their eyes closed throughout the game. They lose their usual frame of reference and have no distractions, only the sound and a free kinesthetic sense of themselves and what their bodies can do in movement.

This is as fascinating an experience for the soundmaker as it is for those who react. Experiment with the different tones and rhythms of your instruments. When you see the effect each instrument produces on the children, allow yourself to respond to them; you'll create a flowing chain of communication in which any one of you can be the initiator. This exchange between the leader and the group is one of the "magic" elements of the game.

After they work on the floor, have the children rise to their knees, then later, to their feet, as they respond to your sounds. Each new level has different facets to explore—new twists and turns and bends. Encourage their exploration of new movement and even say, "Now try things you have never done before!"

Remind them that their movements must relate to the quality and intensity of the sound—so that no one falls with a thud if you tinkle a tambourine! When they stand, the children should be well separated or have their eyes open to avoid accidents. They can rise or fall according to the sounds, as long as they are still when you are silent. Point out though that "still" and "not moving" don't mean "dead"; their stillness should be alert and intent as they listen for the next sound.

The next time you play this game, reverse it: start with a loud bang on a drum. The shock will surprise them into large movements.

MUSIC DESIGNS

Results on many levels, with little effort.

This is a game of many kinds of awareness—awareness of the shape, direction and quality of music, and translation of it into line and color. It is a quiet movement game—at least it starts out quietly.

For this game you need one piece of paper (regular notebook size will do) for each child and several colored crayons. You also need records or tapes. Select three that are quite different from each other in quality; for instance, a Chopin nocturne, a Beatles number, an African drum solo, or a popular folk song.

Explain that you are going to play some music and you want the children to tell you what it sounds like. Does it all stay in the same place, or does it go from high to low? Does it weave in and out and around? Does it move slowly and continuously or does it jump and hop? Tell them that if it hops around, you want them to take their crayons and hop around the paper with them. If the music is smooth and connected, they might draw a line, and as the music travels, their line would travel; if the music goes all over, they would travel all over the paper with their crayons.

After you have played a sampling of music, discussed its qualities and how they might draw it, pass out paper and crayons and play a musical selection they can draw to. Be sure to explain that what they draw is their *own* reaction to the music and it will be different from anyone else's drawing. After the first few seconds they will catch on and go at their drawing with gusto. When the music has stopped, let them show each other their work. Point out features of the work that really followed the music line. The more you show the children and verbalize with them, the more acute their perception becomes.

Now play the music again. Ask the children to stand, hold their drawings with both hands, and looking at their own designs, walk out the patterns they have made.

After they walk through the patterns, play the same music once more. This time encourage the children to move freely to the quality of the drawing, to the way it *feels*. Now they know the pattern of the design, they don't need their papers, they can use their whole bodies to express the music. If the music is jumpy, like "Golliwog's Cakewalk," for example, and they have created jumpy patterns, now they can jump with more than just their feet—with their heads, shoulders, knees. If the music is lyrical, and their patterns are connected, now they can use continuous movements that flow from one part of the body to the other, that stretch and reach and bend.

Now ask the children to turn their papers over, and while you play another musical selection, draw it on the other side of the page. This time, when you play the music the second time, they can move in the pattern and quality of their designs at the same time.

It's a good idea to have the children change colored crayons each time, and if you have enough crayons, give each child at least two. They will use both of them at the same time and may create some really interesting and unusual patterns. The children proudly take their "music designs" home for display and praise, and enjoy "explaining" them.

NAMES IN SPACE

Specific, exact, and demanding, this game starts the children choreographing for themselves.

Ask the children to draw the initial letters of their first names in the air with their index fingers, first as small as they can, then as large as they can. Let them walk the letter in space with just their feet, outlining the shape of the letter; then ask them to run it. Have them start at the end of the letter and trace it in reverse. How about skipping it, or sliding it?

The possibilities are endless: combine two kinds of steps, perhaps a skip and a slide; older children might add a turn at the start or finish. If your group is large, two children with the same name or first initial can work together, starting at opposite ends of the letter and meeting in the middle.

Do it with numbers, too (try birthdays), and you'll have a chance to work with all the basic shapes; 0—the circle; 1—the straight line; 3 and 6—the curve. The number 8 is great fun to play with; get the whole group to walk it out and get the feel of it by leaning into and enjoying each curve. Once the children can walk the shape of the letter or number easily, ask them to add an arm movement as they walk. When they repeat it, ask them to move both arms. The next time, suggest they use just hip movements, and then combine both arms and hips. This requires concentration, as there are many things to think about and co-ordinate, but older children won't have any trouble with it if you add each new complication gradually.

You can do math problems, too—addition and subtraction. Have one child walk a number; add another child who walks a different number, and let a third child walk the sum of the two. You can say it, as the children do it: "Three and four is seven."

RUN A BAKER'S DOZEN!

A run is a run is a run? Not if you add an idea to it.

Here are thirteen different ways to run, and you can use them in any space:

1. *Just run in a circle.*
2. *Run as if you're late for school.*
3. *Run in slow motion.*
4. *Run backwards.* Everyone should run in the same direction, so there are no bumps.
5. *Jet run.* With arms outstretched, lean your wings from side to side, and come in for a landing. Try not to crash!

6. *Run-and-clap.* As you run, clap twice first above your head, then behind your back, then on each side and finally with hands outstretched in front of you.

7. *Clown run.* Make us laugh.

8. *Run-and-stop.* Do eight fast runs and STOP four counts. Each time you stop, freeze in a different position.

9. *Snob run*—As if everything around you is dirty, and you don't like it; put your nose in the air and shake other people's germs off your shoulders.

10. *Thieves' run.* You have a bag of loot. Heave it over your shoulder and sneak away fast. Make sure no one's following you.

11. *Charlie Chaplin run.* On your heels, turn your toes out, and take tiny steps fast. Keep your body stiff.

12. *Top-run.* Like a twirling top, reach your arms to the side, and spin in large steps across the room.

13. *Monster run.* Drag one leg behind you, and reach out your arms to catch a victim.

These are a few "run" possibilities. Feel free to add your own inspirations and ask the children for ideas. You can create an endless number of runs, walks, or sits. Use jumps, hops, skips, turns and gallops. Try adding character and situation ideas. Skip as if it's a beautiful spring day. Jump like a pogo stick going down the street. Run like the spiral in a notebook—start at the top, go down, and then come up again.

7. FASCINATING RHYTHM

ISOLATED RHYTHM

A right-on rhythm game that leads to inventing your own movement.

Write a simple rhythm line. You may want to start with one which looks like this:

Have the children form a circle and sit in it. Clap out the rhythm pattern over and over until they know it well.

"Now do that rhythm pattern only with your head." This time, instead of clapping it, just say "Da, da, dada da; da, da, dah!" as you move your head in rhythm. It is difficult to use *only* your head. Be sure to explain that, and point out that shoulders are not included, nor are any other parts of the body. Heads can move front and back, from side to side and around. Within this range, of course, many different movements are possible.

Next time you work the rhythm line, move only your shoulders. They can shake up and down, move around, and front and back. Again, stress that shoulders are the only moving parts. Do not include your head, or chest, or arms. See what interesting movements you can find!

When you try the rhythm with your arms, use your fingers, wrists, and elbows, but no shoulders.

Stand and use the rhythm with your hips alone. Then use it only with your feet (in place and then moving in space) and finally do it with your entire body.

Then ask the children to go through the sequence as they stand in the circle using the rhythm:

once for the head

once for the shoulders

once for the arms

once for the hips

once for the feet

once for the entire body

As you get to the end of each rhythm line, shout out the next part of the body to be used. Explain that we are moving the rhythm down our bodies, starting from the top. The children will soon remember the sequence and which parts they have already worked.

Next time start the rhythm in reverse with your feet, and work it up your body to your head. At the end, use your entire body.

At this point, allow the children to use any two parts of the body they choose—in combination. This is not at all easy; it requires a great deal of concentration.

For a more swinging and complex beat, try:

or choose your favorite rock, jazz or boogie woogie music, find its basic rhythms and use those as your rhythm lines.

LUNGE AND TOUCH

Encounters in space.

Here is another rhythm line:

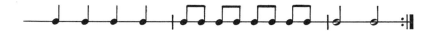

As you read this rhythm line, you can see that the first measure has four walking notes, the second has eight running notes, and the last measure two giant notes. Make those giant notes into lunges.

Ask the children to spread out around the room and walk (in any direction or pattern) the first four notes, run the next eight notes, and then lean toward someone else with each of those two giant lunges. Then repeat the sequence, but this time ask the children not only to lean toward someone, but actually to touch. Try touching hands first—in different positions: clap hands; twist the bodies and touch palms; touch the backs of the hands, slap them. There are many ways to touch hands. Explore them.

Next time, on the lunge, try touching feet; next touch both hands and feet, then touch shoulders. This game leads to involved movement combinations with another person, and opens up many new possibilities.

After you explore "touching" possibilities, change the space of the game. Each time you repeat it, ask the children to go back to where they started, take one jump toward the middle of the room, and begin from that new point. They must not go beyond that point, but must move in toward the center of the circle. Each time they will have less space to work in and will be closer to each other for the lunges. Now instead of touching only one person, you may touch two—or more. The children become more aware of each other, and of their movements in relation to each other. With each start one jump closer, they will soon be moving almost in place. In order to get variety into their movements as space decreases, they will have to move at different levels.

Each time they start, give them a word which describes the character of the next sequence. Use the words like "sassy," "angry," "happy," "mean," "crooked," "beautiful." Make sure the children understand they are to perform the entire rhythm line with this quality—not just the lunges. When the space has been exhausted, ask the children to make up another rhythm line. You can also play this game in reverse. Start the circle close to each other, and move it one step out each time.

NAMES ON 7—JUMP ON 8

Eight counts of "I-AM" in movement.

1
Ask the children to sit in a circle, and beat out eight even counts with both hands on the floor. Have them count aloud as they do it, and then start over again immediately.

2
Now have them accent the seventh count, by beating and saying it louder. Let them repeat this a few times, so they really have the accent of the seventh beat in their bodies.

3
Ask them to shout out their names on the seventh count.

4
Now have the children squat and play the same rhythm, but this time on the seventh count, they jump up in the air with arms lifted, shout out their names and land on the floor on the count of "Eight." Then they start counting from "One" right away without any break.

Now they are ready for the game. Everyone sits in a circle and beats the eight counts without interruption. The first child stands in place and does six sharp movements which tell the group what he or she feels like today. Then the child jumps up in the air on "Seven," shouts out his or her name, and falls to the floor on "Eight." The next person is already up and moving on "One." Continue the game until everyone in the circle has had a turn.

Next time you play this game, before it starts, call out a word, such as "proud," "scared," "flippant," "nasty," "sweet," and all the children must perform their movements with that image.

This movement game has a momentum and spirit that carries it through to the end with excitement and great satisfaction.

WAYS TO INVENT MOVEMENT

Whatever movement games you start with, you can vary them, intensify them, make them more dramatic, different, or original by changing only one element. If you want to invent your own movement games, take any basic game from this book—or any other—and try adding one of the concepts listed here. You may come out with an entirely new activity and one that is unique and particularly suited to the group.

1. Levels—Movements can be performed at standing level, down low, on the floor or in the air. Don't forget all the levels in between. Try a standing game sitting, a running game crawling, a floor game on your toes.

2. Dynamics—Is the movement smooth or sharp—percussive or sustained —light or heavy—erratic—strong—energetic or droopy? Limit a game to one quality of movement, and then perhaps change it in the middle.

3. Rhythmic Variation—Try the game slow or fast or in any combination, such as s-l-o-w-s-l-o-w-fastfastfastfast. Combine moving with periods of "freeze."

4. Direction—Whatever it is, try it backwards! You can also move sidewards or in a zig-zag pattern, or face forward but walk on a diagonal. You can combine directions: gallop forwards, for instance, while you reach your hands behind you, or slide to one side while your body bends the opposite way.

5. Self-Accompaniment—Combine sounds with movement. Cluck your tongue, snap fingers, clap hands, stamp on anything. If you are working with older children who catch on quickly, try syncopating the sounds so that they don't coincide with the rhythm, so that sounds and movements go at a different pace. This requires much concentration.

6. Music or Rhythm Accompaniment—Use a different beat or music to change the mood, to add another dimension, to change the "quality" of the situation.

7. Dramatic Ideas—Add an image. Instead of just skipping, skip down the street with the wind pushing you. Instead of just jumping aimlessly, let a frog jump from one lily pad to another. Take the basic gallop, add to it the idea of cowboys stalking Indians, or settlers chasing cattle rustlers. When you add an image, every movement becomes far more intense and interesting. You can add a feeling (hot, cold, sad), an idea (blasting off, bubbling up), a character (animal or human), or a desire for something special (escape from danger, need to hide, to make people laugh). A run is never so fast (or so unself-conscious) as when it is "away" from something. A roll is freer and smoother when a "pig" does it. The possibilities are unlimited.

Index